A FAR SIDE COLLECTION
UNNATURAL SELECTIONS

Other Books in The Far Side Series

The Far Side
Beyond The Far Side
In Search of The Far Side
Bride of The Far Side
Valley of The Far Side
It Came From The Far Side
~~Moby Dick~~
Hound of The Far Side
The Far Side Observer
Night of the Crash-Test Dummies
Wildlife Preserves
Wiener Dog Art

Anthologies

The Far Side Gallery
The Far Side Gallery 2
The Far Side Gallery 3

Retrospective

The PreHistory of The Far Side:
  A 10th Anniversary Exhibit

A FAR SIDE COLLECTION

UNNATURAL SELECTIONS

BY GARY LARSON

Andrews and McMeel
A Universal Press Syndicate Company
Kansas City

ISBN: 0-8362-1881-7

Library of Congress Catalog Card Number: 91-73171

Printed on recycled paper.

The watercoloring in this book was done by Donna Pickert-Korris;
the gray washes by Jerry McKeehan.

Saturday mornings in cockroach households

"I'm afraid it's bad news, Mr. Griswold. . . . The lab
results indicate your body cavity is stuffed with a
tasty, bread-like substance."

New York, 1626: Chief of the Manhattan Indians
addresses his tribe for the last time.

The crew of the Starship Enterprise encounters the floating head of Zsa Zsa Gabor.

Lemmings on vacation

At the international meeting of the
Didn't Like *Dances With Wolves* Society

"Uh-oh, Bob, the dog's on fire. . . . I think it's your turn
to put him out."

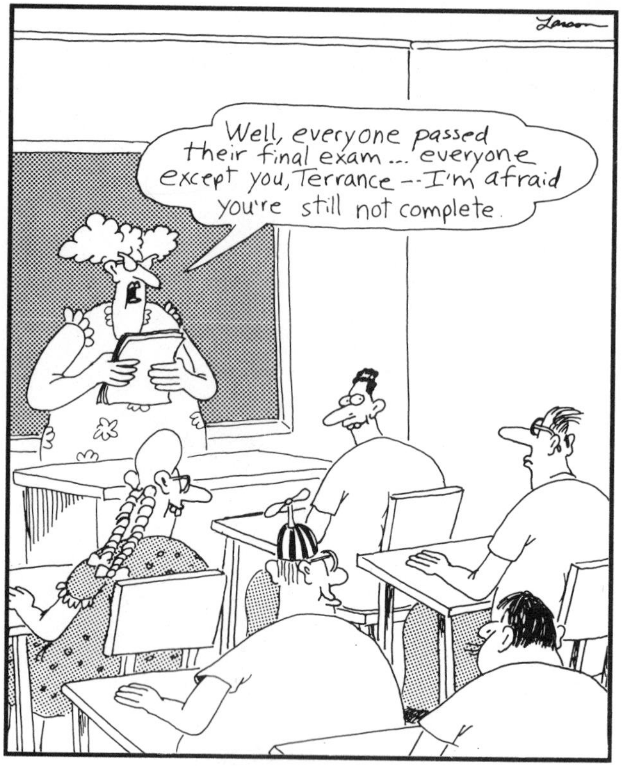
Well, everyone passed their final exam ... everyone except you, Terrance -- I'm afraid you're still not complete.

Fool school

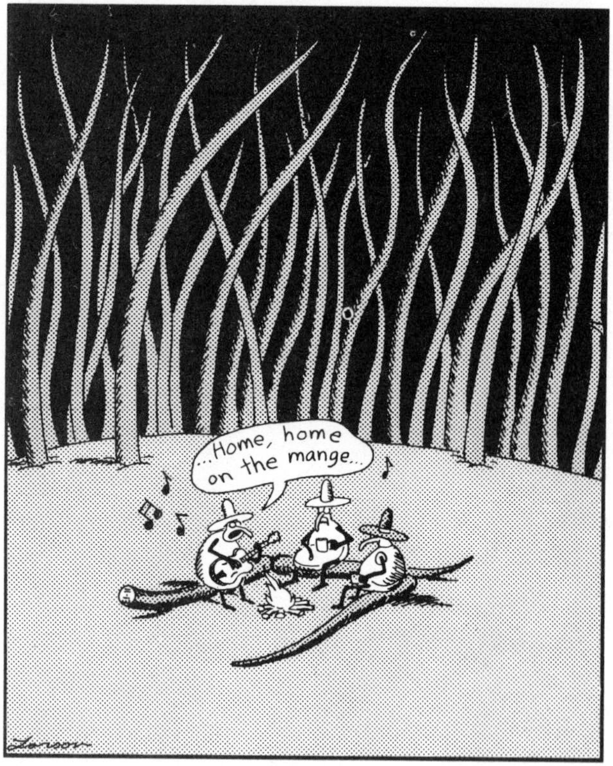
...Home, home on the mange...

Fleaboys

"Hey! What's that clown think he's doing?"

It was foolish for Russell to approach the
hornets' nest in the first place, but his timing
was particularly bad.

11

His rifle poised, Gus burst through the door, stopped, and listened. Nothing but the gentle sound of running water and the rustling of magazines could be heard. The trail, apparently, had been false.

Ghost newspapers

Although nervous, the Dickersons were well-received by this tribe of unique headhunters. It was Pooki, regrettably, that was to bear the brunt of their aggression.

Innovative concepts in exposing city kids to nature

"Wait a minute, friends . . . Frank Stevens in marketing—you all know Frank—has just handed me a note . . ."

"There he is, Stan! . . . On that birch tree, second branch from the top, and chattering away like crazy! . . . I tell you—first come the squirrels and then come the squirrel guns."

The fate of Don King's great-great-grandfather

16

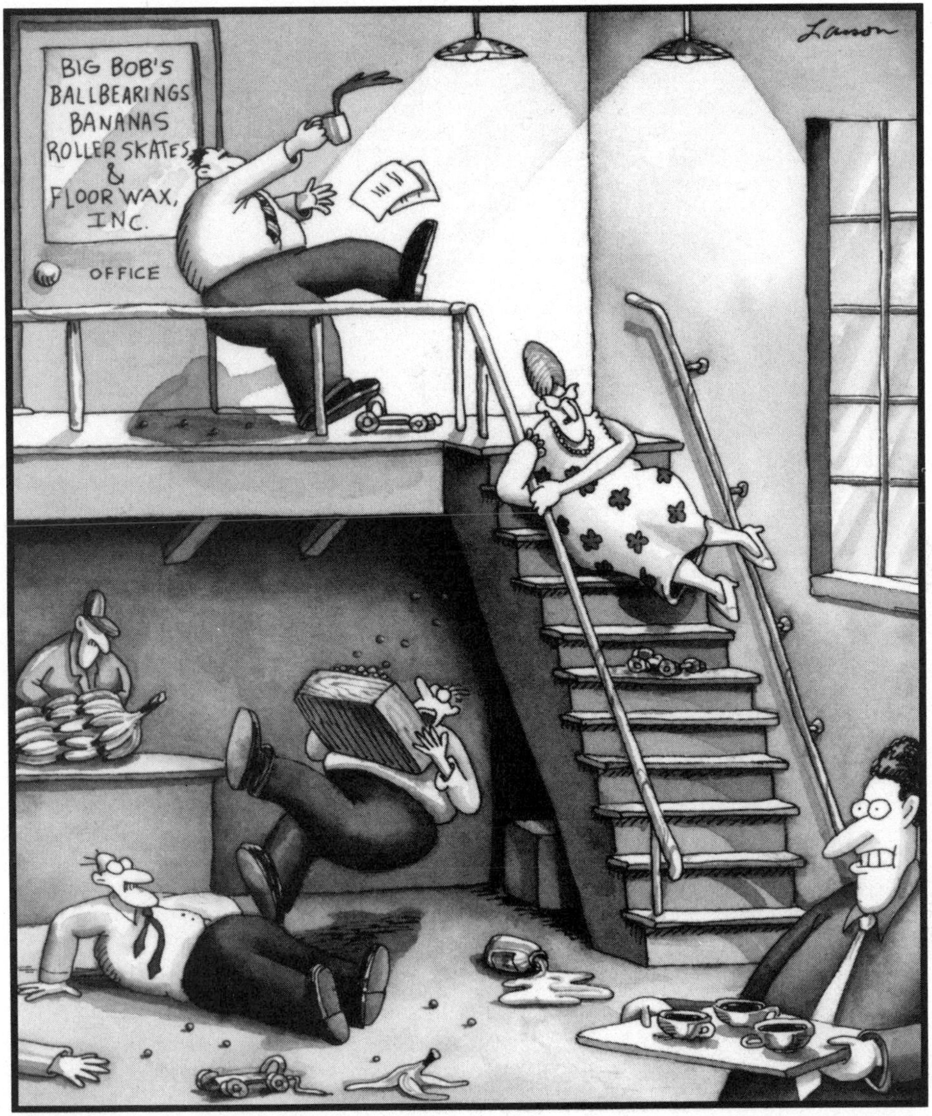
BIG BOB'S
BALLBEARINGS
BANANAS
ROLLER SKATES
&
FLOOR WAX,
INC.
OFFICE

"Oh, man! You must be looking for 'Apartment
3-G,' 'Mary Worth,' or one of those other
'serious' cartoons."

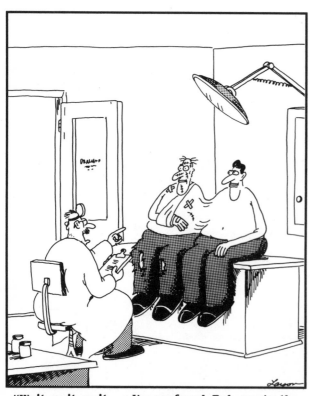

"Wait, wait, wait . . . I'm confused. Bob, *you're* the
one who's claiming your Siamese twin, Frank,
changes into a werewolf every full moon?"

18

"Don't worry, Jimmy—they're just actors . . . and that's not real ketchup."

19

The dam bursts.

"Well, what d'ya know! . . . *I'm* a follower, too!"

20

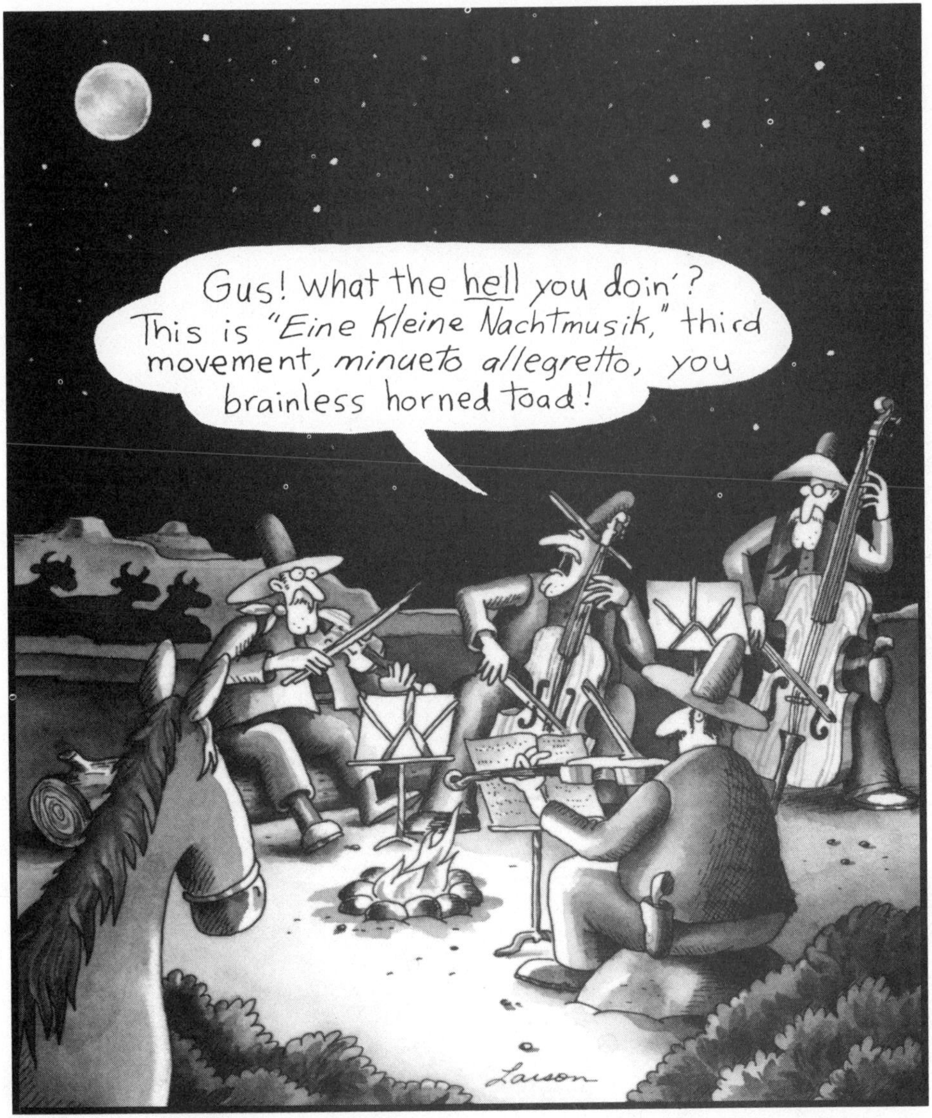
Gus! what the hell you doin'? This is "Eine Kleine Nachtmusik," third movement, minueto allegretto, you brainless horned toad!
Larson

Cattle drive quartets

"Good heavens, John! Call someone! . . . The
entire basement looks dry!"

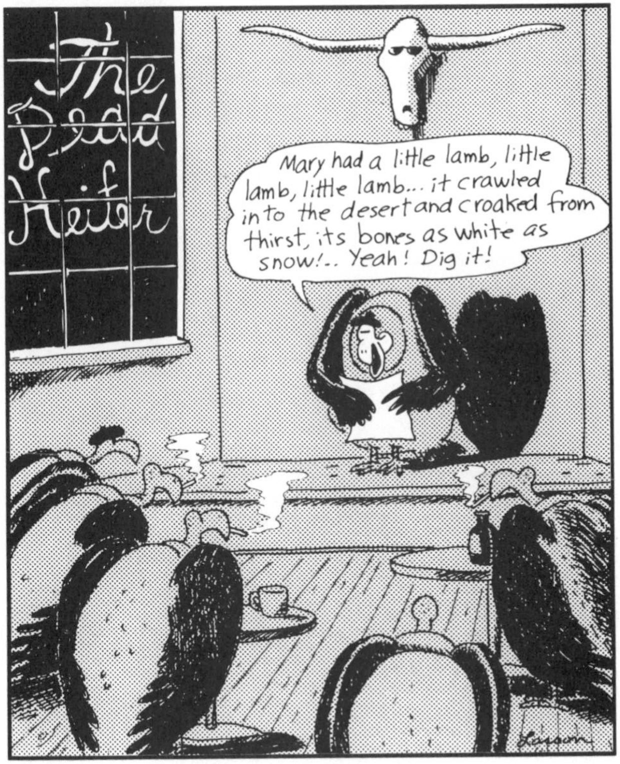
The Dead Heifer
Mary had a little lamb, little lamb, little lamb... it crawled into the desert and croaked from thirst, its bones as white as snow!.. Yeah! Dig it!
Larson
Buzzard beakniks

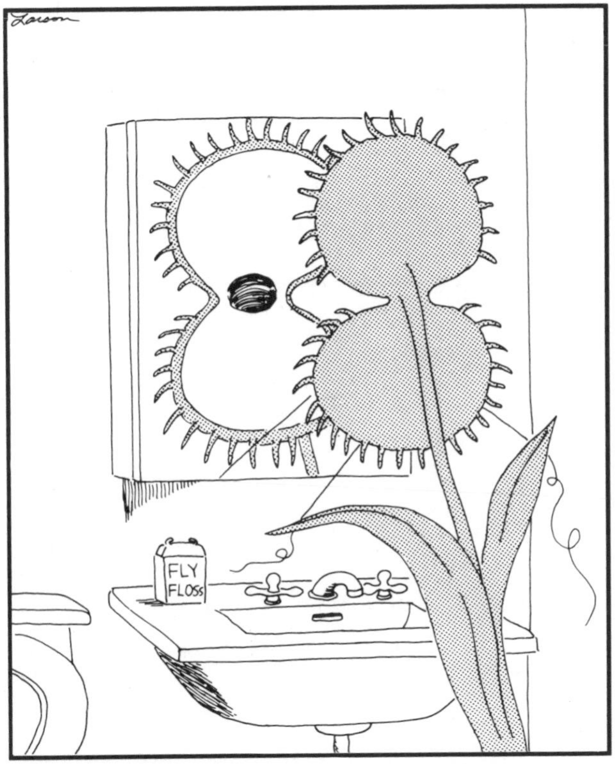
Larson
FLY FLOSS

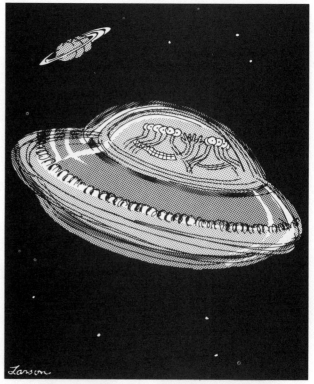

Another photograph from the Hubble telescope

Larson
BLAM!

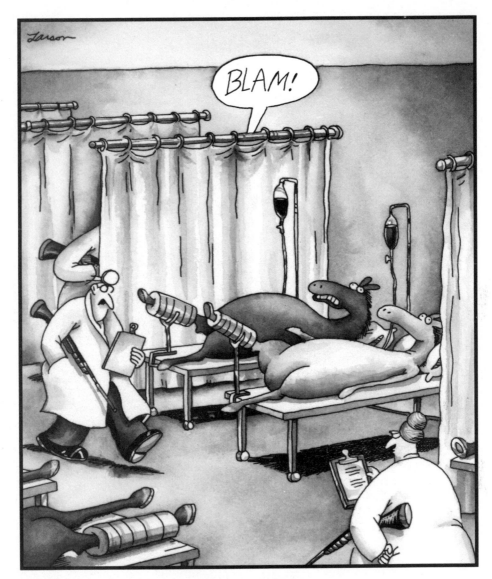

Horse hospitals

"The carnage out here is terrible, Sandy . . .
feathers everywhere you—Oh, here we go! The
Animal Control Officer is leading the so-called
Chicken Coop Three away at this very moment."

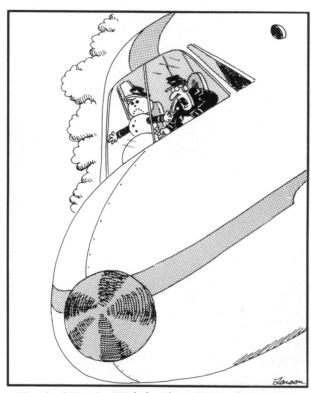

"Mayday! Mayday! This is Flight 97! I'm in trouble!
. . . My second engine's on fire, my landing gear's
jammed, and my worthless copilot's frozen up!"

"Oh, for the love of—there goes Henry! . . . Rita, you're closest to him—give that c-clamp about a quarter turn, will ya?"

27

Hooting excitedly, primitive scientists Thak and
Gork try out their new "Time Log."

"Take a good, long look at this. . . . We don't know
what it is, but it's the only part of the buffalo
we don't use."

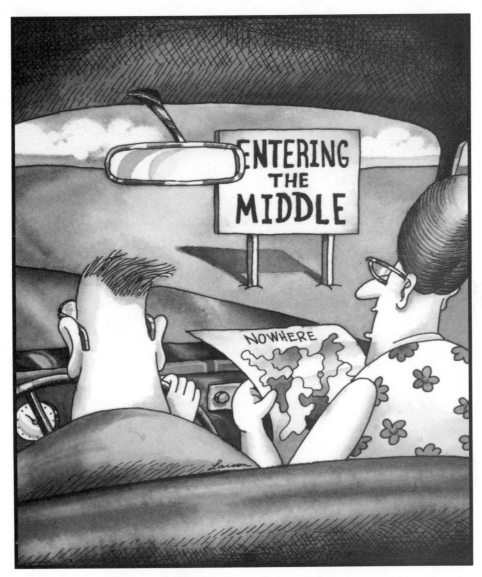

"Well, this is just going from bad to worse."

In sudden disgust, the three lionesses realized
they had killed a tofudebeest—one of the
Serengeti's obnoxious health antelopes.

Hopeful parents

"C'mon! Keep those stomachs over the handle! Let the fat do the work! . . . That's it!"

Aardogs

The party-goers were enjoying themselves immensely—unaware that, across the street in the shadows, a killer waited.

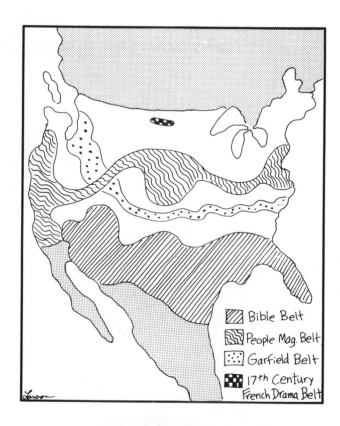

Bible Belt
People Mag. Belt
Garfield Belt
17th Century French Drama Belt

Early but unsuccessful practical jokes

The class was quietly doing its lesson when
Russell, suffering from problems at home,
prepared to employ an attention-getting device.

"Barbara, you just have to come over and see all
my eggs. The address is: Doris Griswold, 5 feet 4
inches, 160 pounds, brown eyes—I'm in her hair."

"Listen—I bought these here yesterday, and the dang things won't stop squeaking!"

"Step back, Loretta! . . . It's a red-hot poker!"

Danook shows off his Swiss Army Rock.

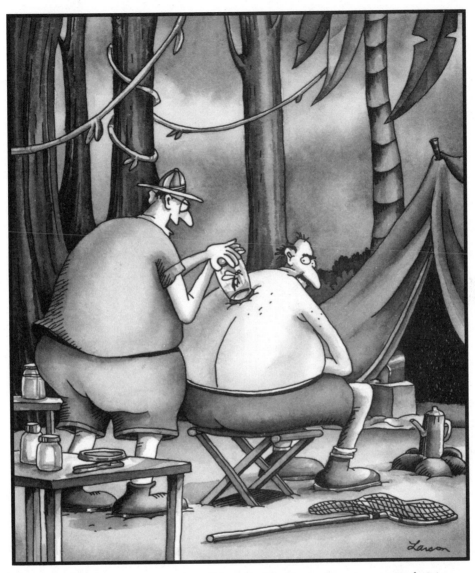

"Got him, Byron! It's something in the *Vespula* genus, all right—
and ooooweeeee does he look mad!"

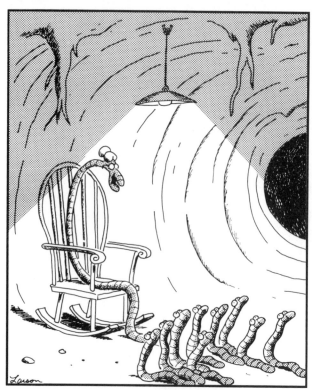

"That story again? . . . Well, one stormy night,
when the whole family was asleep, your
grandfather quietly rose from his bed, took an ax,
and made alllllllll you little grandkids."

"Oh, wait, Doreen—don't sit there. . . . That chair's just not safe."

Innocent and carefree, Stuart's left hand didn't know what the right was doing.

"Hey, I'm *trying* to pass the potatoes! . . . Remember, my forearms are just as useless as yours!"

Front porch forecasters

Gus saw them when he crested the hill: snakes.
Three of them, basking on the road.
Probably diamondbacks.

Kid shows that bombed

**"What? You've met someone else?
What are you saying? . . . Oh, my God!
It's not what's-his-name, is it?"**

Math phobic's nightmare

Freudian slide

Lizard thugs

Charlie Parker's private hell

Insect game shows

"Oh, professor. . . . Did I tell you I had another out-of-head experience last night?"

Saving on transportation costs, some pioneers were known to head west on covered skates.

"Ticks, fleas . . . Ticks, fleas . . ."

"Just ignore him. That's our rebellious young calf Matthew — he's into wearing leather clothes just for the shock value."

The Evolution of Life on Earth

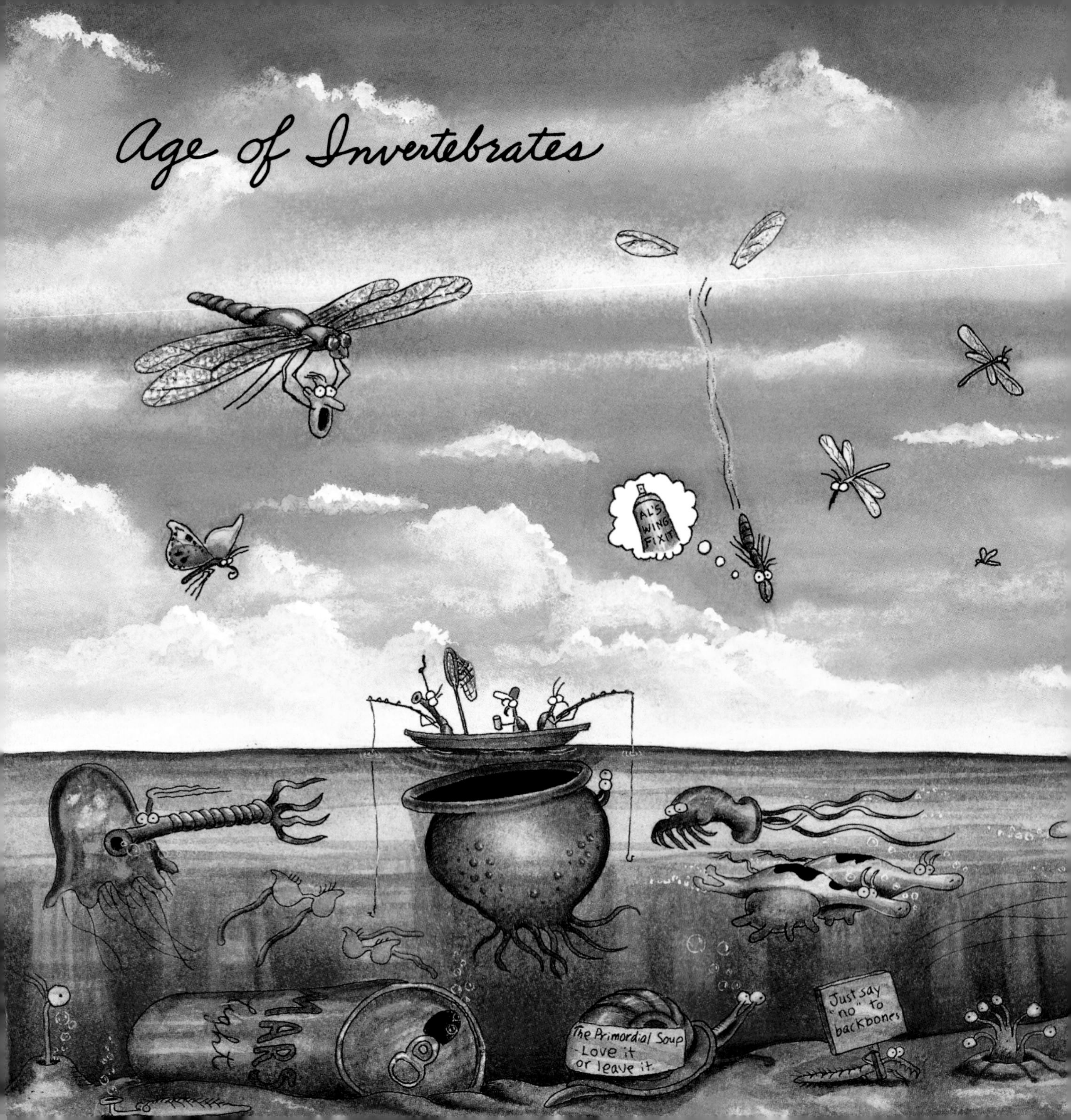
Age of Invertebrates
AL'S WING FIXIT
MARS light
The Primordial Soup - Love it or leave it
Just say "no" to backbones

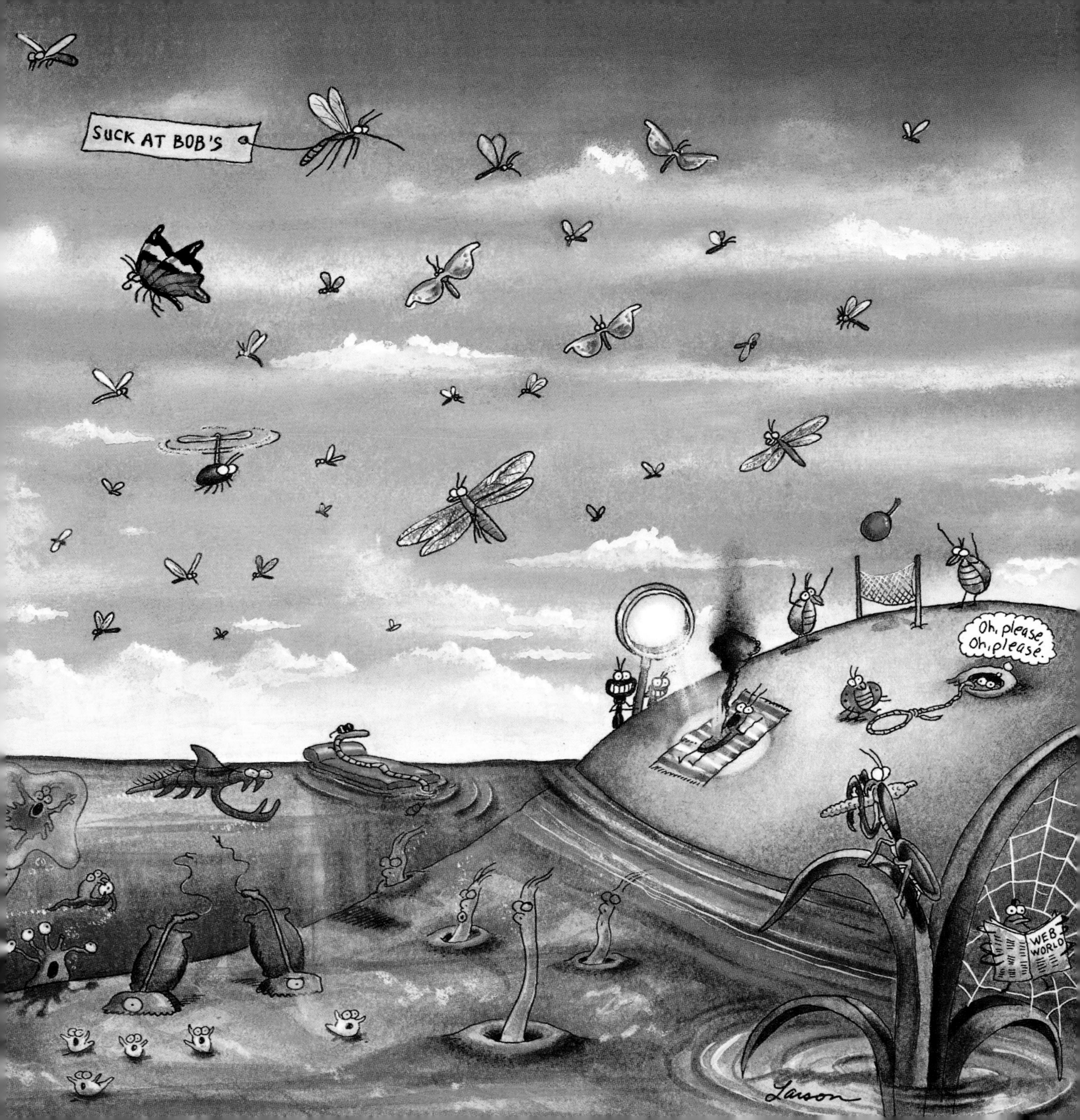
SUCK AT BOB'S
Oh, please, Oh, please.
WEB WORLD
Larson

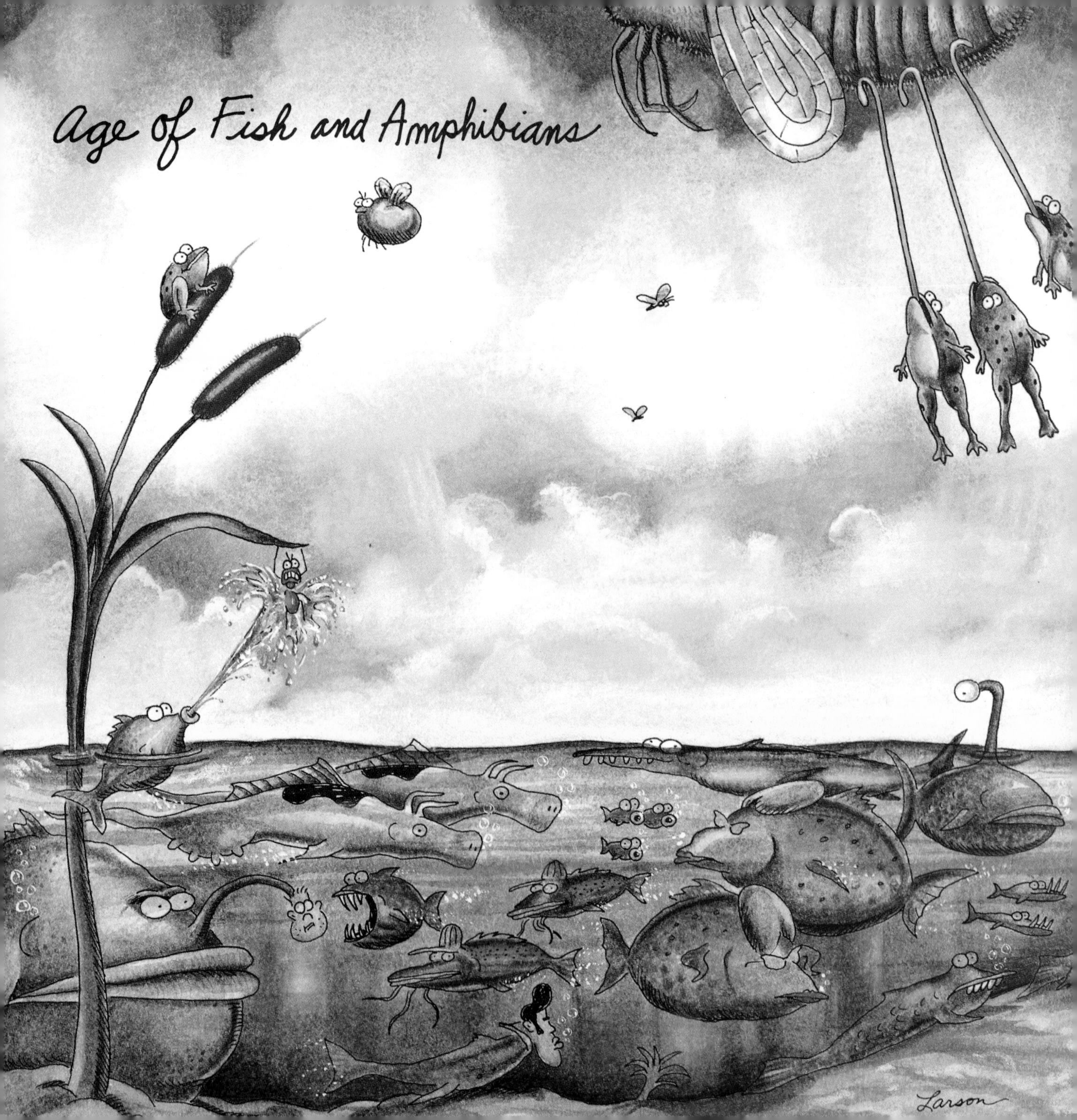
Age of Fish and Amphibians
Larson

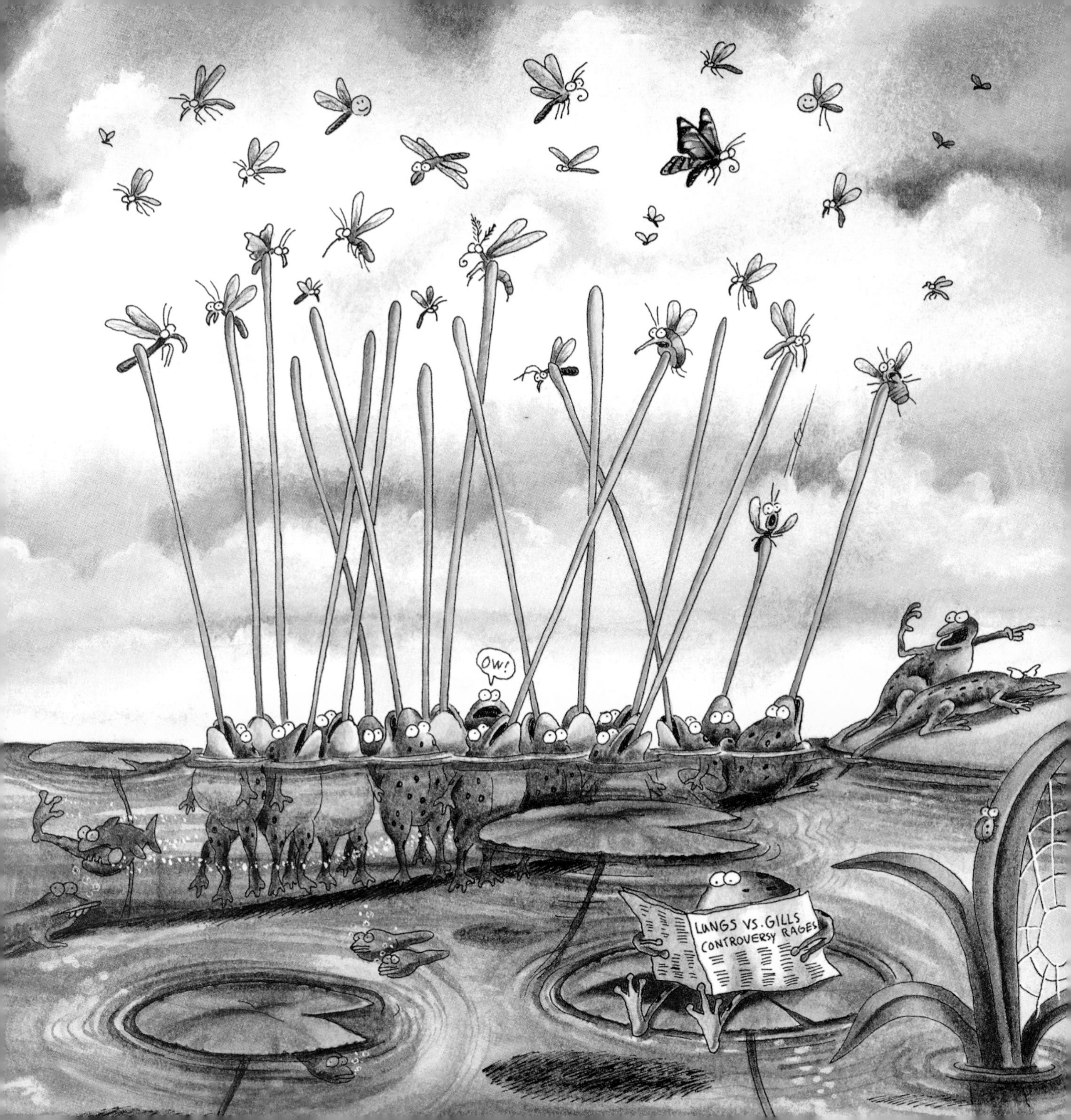
OW!
LUNGS VS. GILLS
CONTROVERSY RAGES

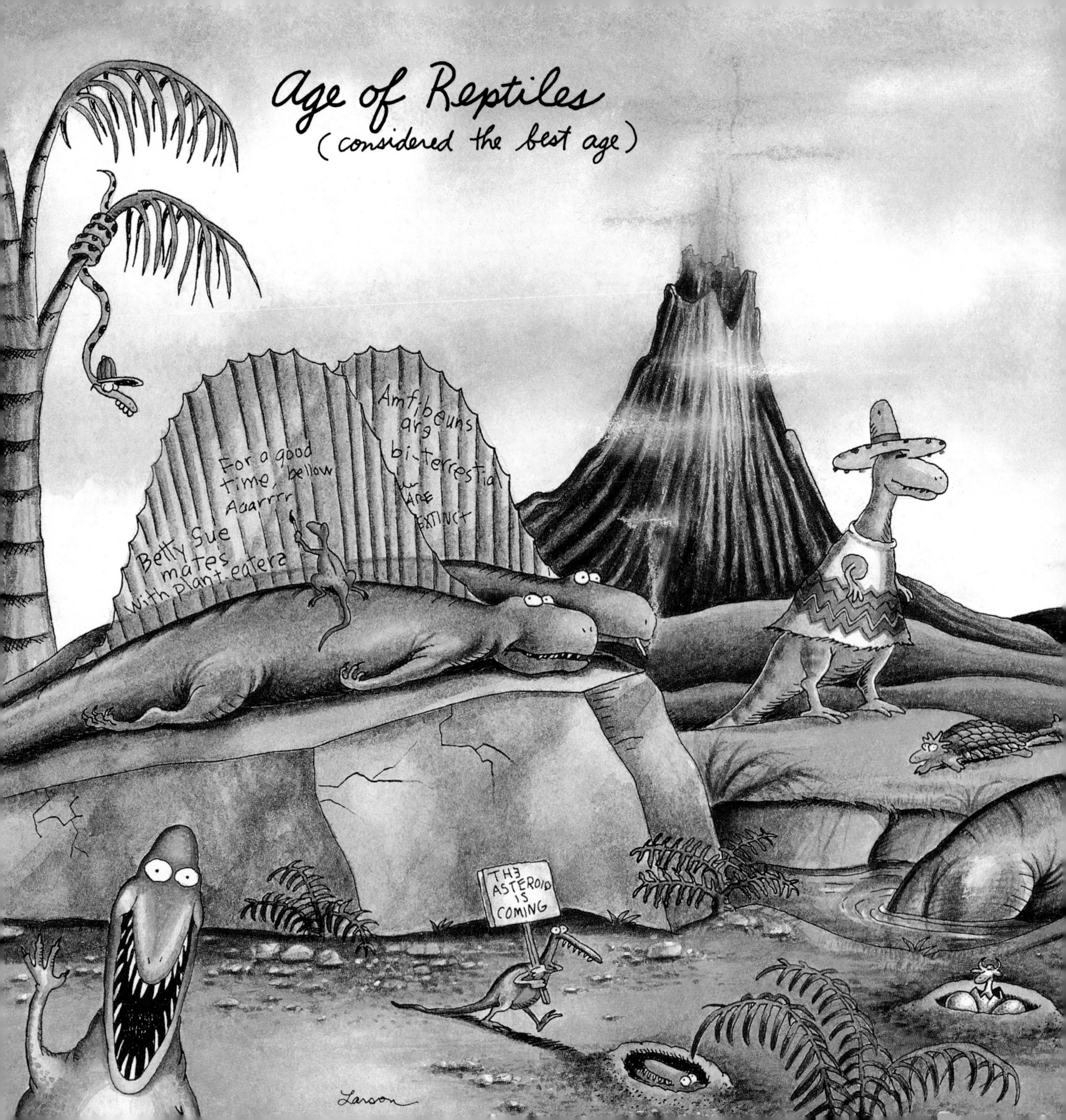
Age of Reptiles
(considered the best age)
For a good time, bellow Aaarrrr
Betty Sue mates with plant-eaters
Amfibeuns are bi-terrestia
ARE EXTINCT
THE ASTEROID IS COMING
Larson

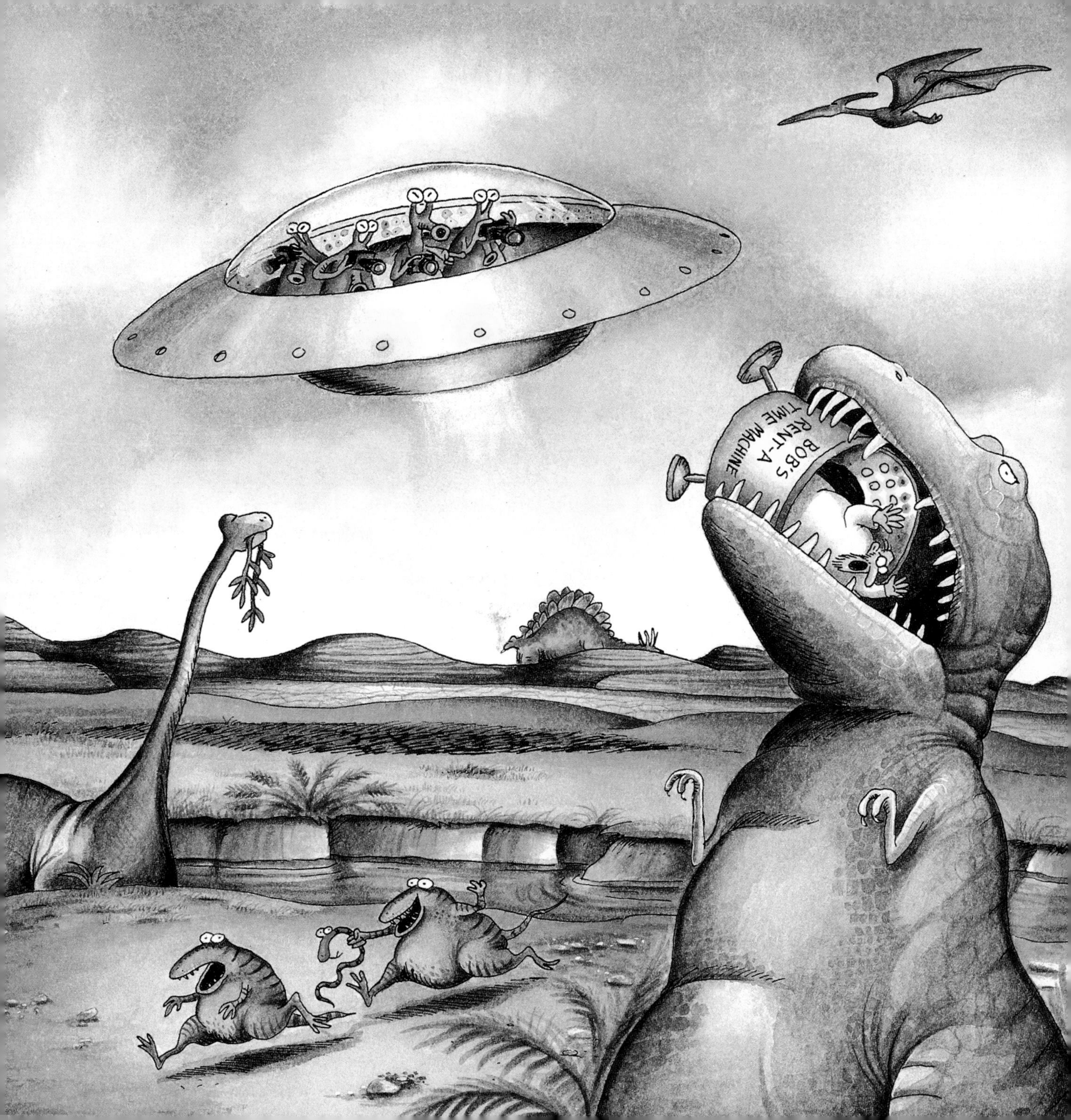
BOB'S
RENT-A
TIME MACHINE

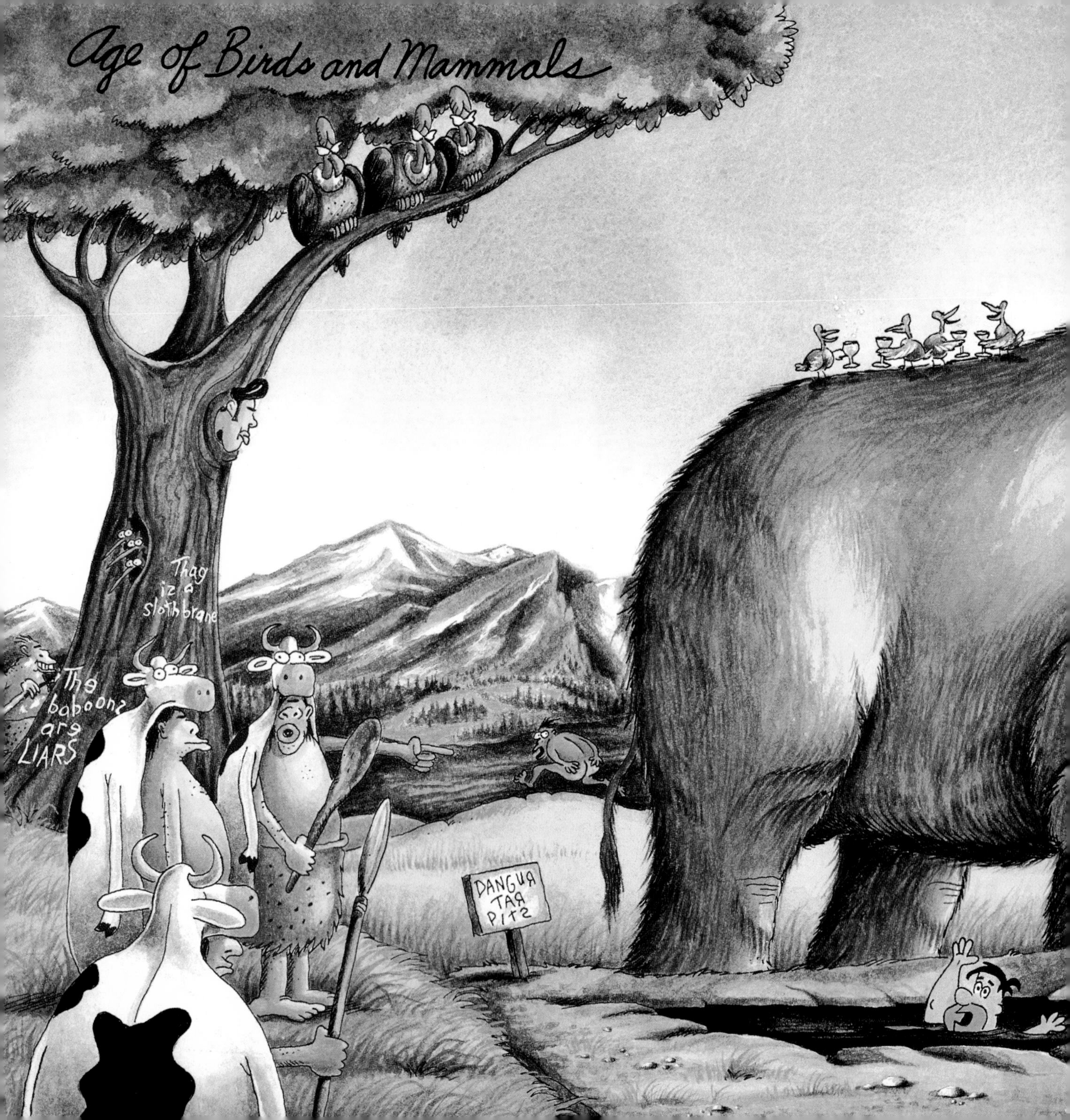

Age of Birds and Mammals
Thag iz a slothbrane
The baboonz are LIARS
DANGUR TAR PITS

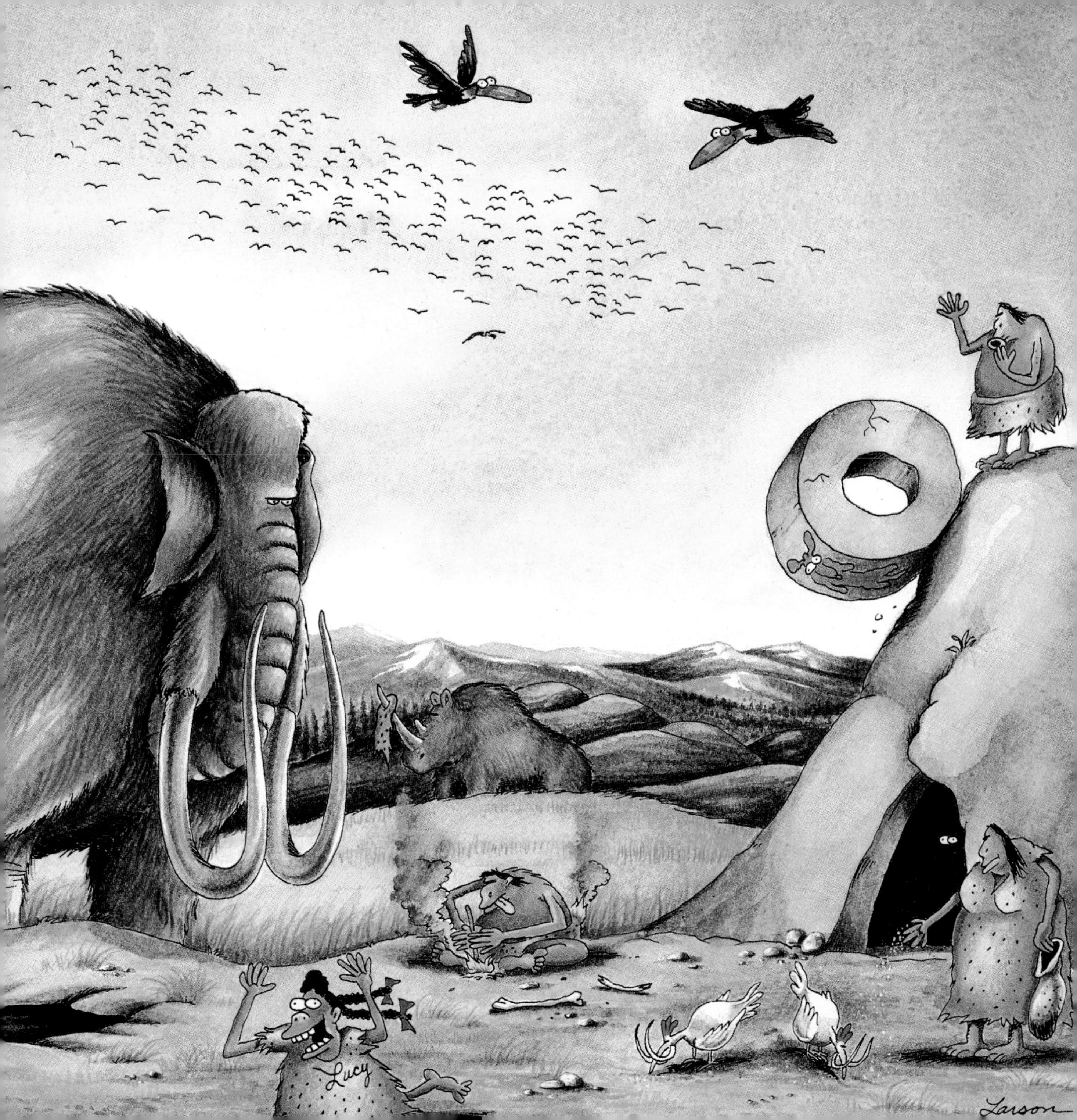
Lucy
Larson

The Future
(I'm sure of it.)
MRS. LOW'S
"Long-Lasting"
The
UDDERPLACE
Bovinnie's
HEIFERS!
HEIFERS!
HEIFERS!
THE
COW CATCHER
NOW
PLAYING:
101
DEAD
MATADORS
Lulu Jones
has hoof
and mouth
Larson
BARN-
LESS
EAT
HAY
& DIE
APPEARING
AT THE
BLOWFLY TAVERN
THE
DEATH CALVES
SAME
MANURE,
DIFFERENT
DAY
alfalfa breath
FRANK MOODY HAS
OATS FOR BRAINS
(Moofia staff car)

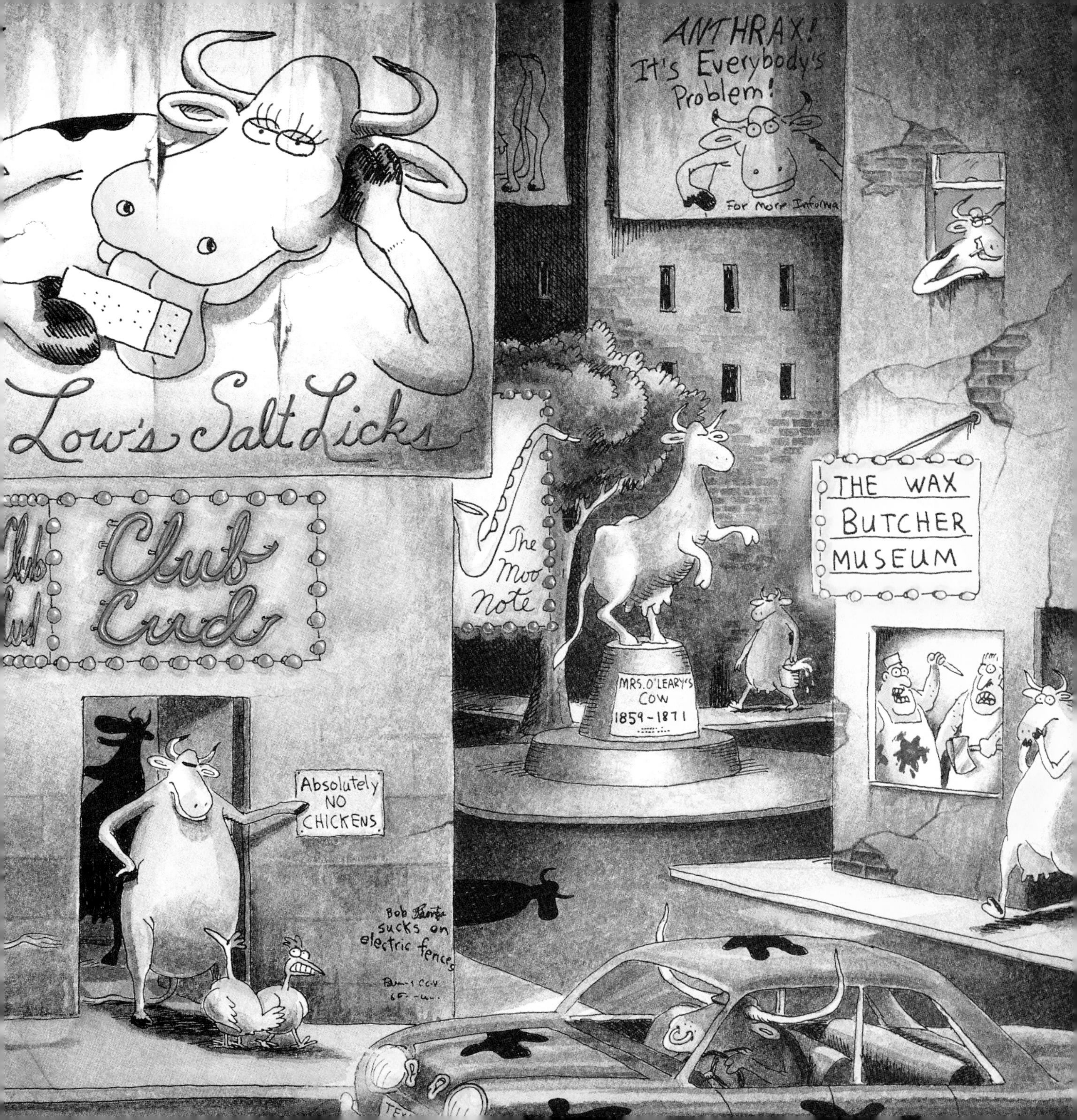

ANTHRAX! It's Everybody's Problem!
Low's Salt Licks
Club Cud
The Moo Note
MRS. O'LEARY'S COW 1859-1871
THE WAX BUTCHER MUSEUM
Absolutely NO CHICKENS
sucks on electric fences

Professor Lundquist, in a seminar on compulsive thinkers, illustrates his brain-stapling technique.

Every hour on the hour, a huge truck, made
entirely of pressed ham, lumbers its way across
Dog Heaven—and all the car chasers can decide for
themselves whether or not to participate.

"Look at this shirt, Remus! You can zip-a-dee-doo-
dah all day long for all I care, but you keep that
dang Mr. Bluebird off your shoulder!"

The Ty-D-bol family at home

"Oh, the whole flower bed is still in shock. He was
such a quiet butterfly—kept to himself mostly."

"Aaaaaa! There goes another batch of eggs, Frank!
. . . No wonder this nest was such a deal."

You never see it coming.

"Yeah, Clem, I hurt. But y'know, it's a *good* kind of hurt."

"Make a note of this, Muldoon. . . . The wounds
seem to be caused by bird shot . . . big bird shot."

"You just take your prey, slip 'em into the flex-o-
tube, flip the switch, and the Mr. Coils o'Death
takes over."

"Whoa! Whoa! Whoa! . . . You're in my favorite
chair again, Carl."

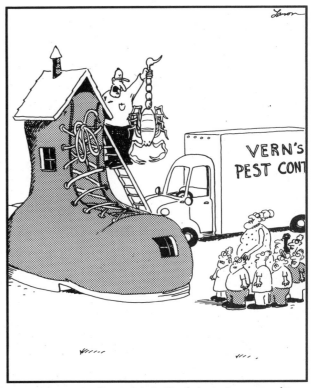

"OK, ma'am—it's dead. In the future, however, it's
always a good idea to check your shoe each time
you and the kids return home."

Houdini's final undoing

**Nature films that Disney test-marketed
but never released.**

George Washington: general, president, visionary, break dancer.

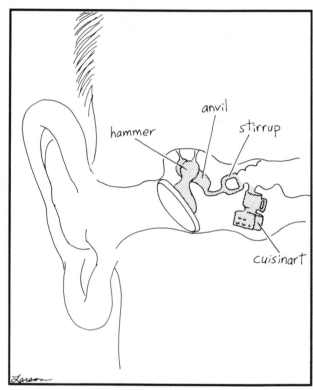

Professor Harold Rosenbloom's diagram of the middle ear, proposing his newly discovered fourth bone.

Buffalo, N.Y., November 2-5: The annual convention of the Big Galoot Society of America.

"Oh, my! Cindy! This looks exquisite! . . . And look, Frank—isn't that a cheeseball stuffed in its mouth?"

Far Side Lite: Not funny, but better for you.

February 22, 1952: Veterinarians attempt the first skunk de-scenting operation.

The hazards of teaching young Neanderthals

Misunderstanding his employees' screams of "Simmons has lost his marbles," Mr. Wagner bursts from his office for the last time.

The growing field of animal liposuction

God makes the snake

A day in the Invisible Man's household

Baby toys and gifts to avoid this Christmas

"You know, I used to like this hobby. . . .
But shoot! Seems like *everybody's* got
a rock collection."

What really happened to Tinkerbell

"Ben—what d'ya say we turn the power off for a while and let the little guy roam around?"

Each time the click beetle righted itself, Kyle would flip it over again—until something went dreadfully wrong.

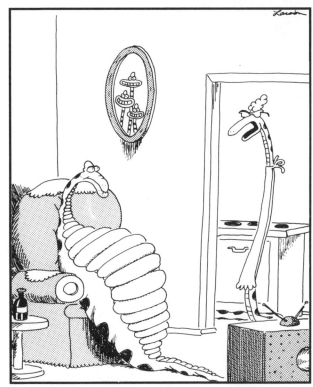

"Joe! You went and ate the pig I was going to serve this evening to the MacIntyres? . . . Well, you just disgorge it—it should still be OK."

"Zak! Don't eat parsley! Just for looks!"

The four basic personality types

"My God! It *is* Professor Dickle! . . . Weinberg,
see if you can make out what the devil
he was working on, and the rest of you get back
to your stations."

Wiener dog distribution centers

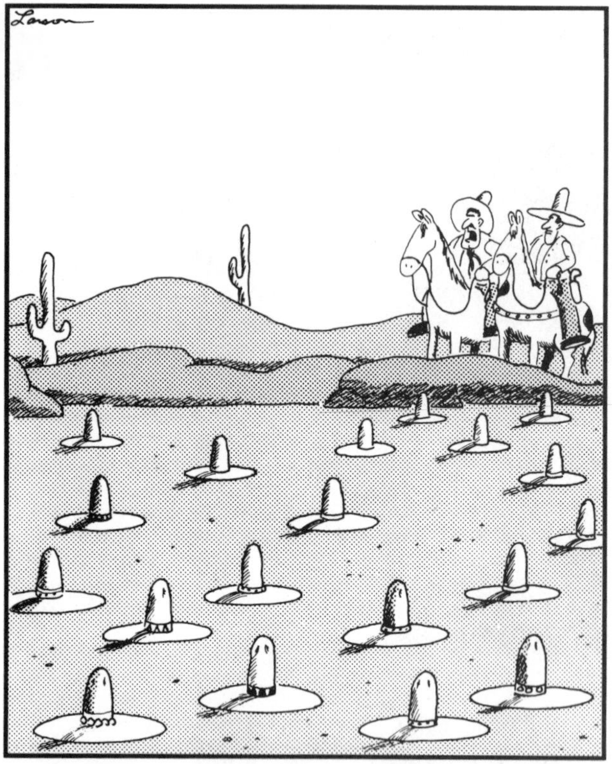
Larson

"We must be careful, Cisco! . . . Thees could be the eenfamous Queek Sand Beds of Chihuahua."

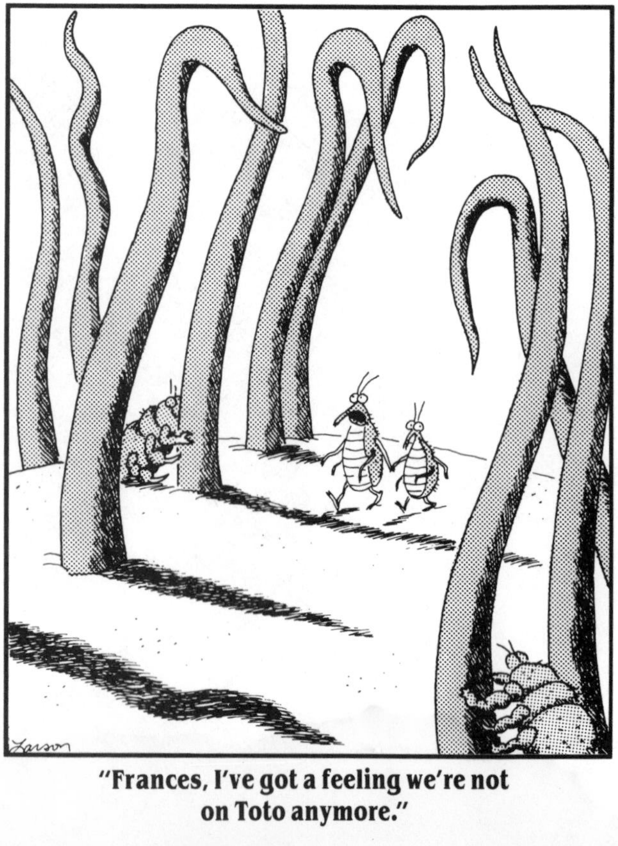
Larson

"Frances, I've got a feeling we're not on Toto anymore."

And so it went, night after night, year after year.
In fact, the Hansens had been in a living hell
ever since that fateful day the neighbor's
"For Sale" sign had come down and a
family of howler monkeys had moved in.

Far away, on a hillside, a very specialized breed of
dog heard the cry of distress.

Inside a nuclear power plant

"Well, we could go back to my place, but you have to understand—I'm *serious* when I say it's just a hole in the wall."

However, there was no question that, on the south side of the river, the land was ruled by the awesome *Tyrannosaurus Mex*.

"Oh God, George! Stop! . . . Stop the car! I've got
another migration headache!"

"Dave! Ain't that your horse that kid
is messin' with?"

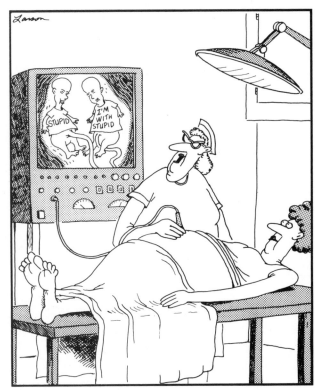

"There you go, Mrs. Eagen—you can clearly see
both twins on the monitor."

Leon Redbone's workout video

87

"Criminy! Talk about overstaying your welcome!
. . . John, open the door and turn the porch light
on—see if that gets rid of them."

The squirrels of Central Park

Suddenly, two bystanders stuck their heads
inside the frame and ruined one of the
funniest cartoons ever.

As the small band of hunter-gatherers sat around cleaning their weapons, one made the mistake of looking at his club straight on.

Suddenly, to Rodney's horror, the police arrived with nerd-sniffing dogs.

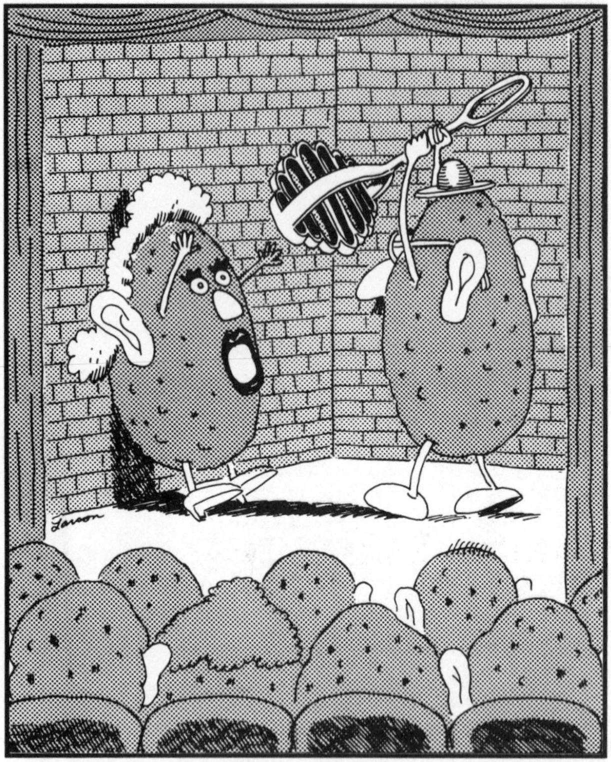
Larson
Masher films

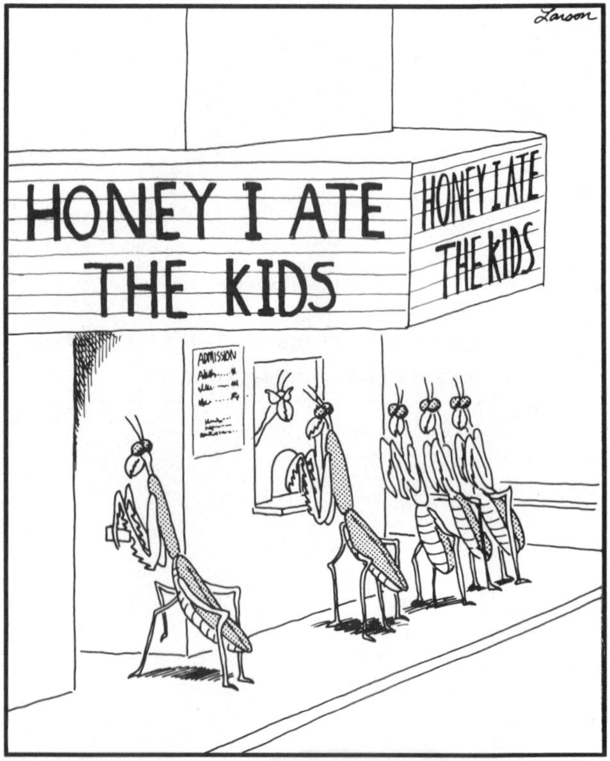
Larson
HONEY I ATE
THE KIDS
HONEY I ATE
THE KIDS
ADMISSION

"The guy creeps me out, Zeena. Sure, he looks like he's just minding his own business—but he always keeps that one eye on my house."

"Well, it's a delicate situation, sir. . . .
Sophisticated firing system, hair-trigger
mechanisms, and Bob's wife just left him last
night, so you *know* his mind's not into this."

The Secret Elephant Aerial Grounds

Famous patrons of Chez Rotting Carcass

The birth of head-hunting

And with Johnny's revelation, Mr. Goodman's
popularity in the neighborhood
suddenly plummeted.

"Wait, Morrison! . . . It's OK—those are
jungle *triangles*!"

"Idiot! . . . You're standing on my foot!"

"Say, Anthony, this looks like a
pleasant little place."

"No, no, no! . . . That regular rock!
Me need Phillips!"

Forbidden Fruit

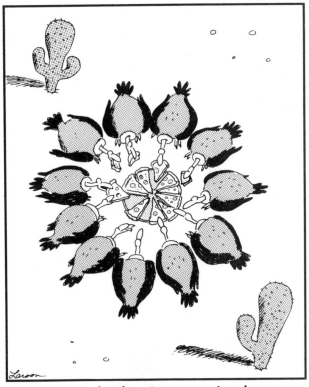

Perspectives in nature we rarely enjoy

Although history has long forgotten them, Lambini & Sons are generally credited with the Sistine Chapel floor.

"Who are we kidding, Luke? We know this is going to be just another standoff."

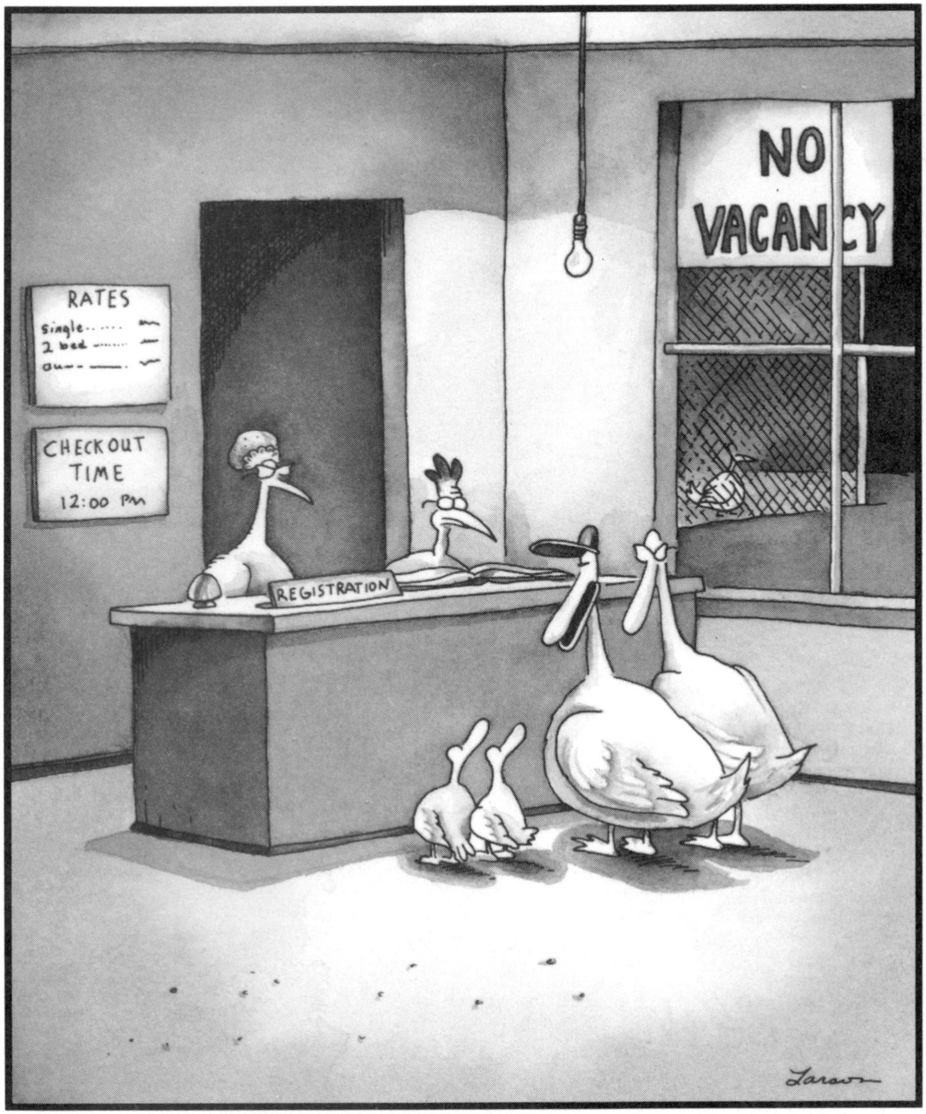
RATES
single
2 bed
CHECKOUT TIME 12:00 PM
REGISTRATION
NO
VACAN CY
Larson

"Sorry, kids—they've got cable, but no pond."

Primitive UFOs

On what was to be his last day on the job, Gus is caught asleep at the switch.

Centipede parking lots

"Well, scratch No. 24. He did pretty good,
though—right up to the jet engine test."

In the corner, Vance was putting the move on two females—unaware that his fake hood had begun to slip.

Fish funerals

Proving once again that the most dangerous animals in the jungle are not always the biggest, the arrow-poison frogs danced victoriously on Steinberg's face.

Llamas at home

Medieval pickup battles

"Now, this is our dead beetle room, and some of these babies are 50 times an ant's body weight. . . . 'Course, we'll want to start *you* out on dried ladybugs."